JOY PIANO

Bring Music to Life

COMPLETE PIANO SCALES

In all the Major and Minor Keys
Two Octave scales

Joy Piano

📍 Seattle, Washington, USA

✉ Joypianoseattle@gmail.com

💻 Amazon.com/author/joypiano

📷 Instagram.com/joypianomusic

Created by:
Moonhee Kim

ISBN: 9798431271366
Imprint: Independently published

TABLE OF CONTENTS

Major and Minor scales, including enharmonic scales

Why do you need to practice and study "Scales"?

Piano scales are an important part of developing your playing skills, they greatly help you improve your awareness of tones and your knowledge of all the keys. Plus, they help you develop fast, nimble fingers and teach you how to move your thumb efficiently, which is the foundation of all piano playing.

Not only will this book help you develop coordination between your hands, but it will also develop finger strength, a strong sense of rhythm, clarity, and speed, which are all important for playing the piano.

What are music "Scales"?

Scales are a group of notes, in alphabetical order, that are a specific distance apart from each other.

In this book, you will learn two basic scales, major and minor. Major scales were judged to be brighter and cheerful sounds, while minor scales were judged to be darker and sadder.

What is a half step and whole step?

A half step is the smallest interval between any two adjacent keys. A whole step is two half steps in either direction.

Half step

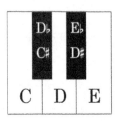

Ex) C to C# is a half step

Whole step

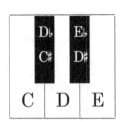

Ex) C to D or D to C is a whole step.

What is a major scale?

A major scale is an ordered collection of half steps and whole steps. Half steps are between the 3rd and 4th, and the 7th and 8th degrees, and whole steps are between the other adjacent degrees. Major scales are named after their first note.

Ex) C major scale

Scale degree :

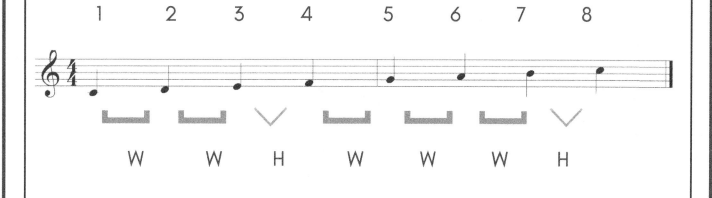

What is a minor scale?

A minor scale is built on the 6th scale degree of the relative major scale. For example, the 6th scale degree of C major scale is "A" , and its relative minor scale is A minor.

There are three different types of minor scales: Natural, harmonic, and melodic.

1. Natural minor

Each note of a natural minor is identical to its relative major scale, but the first note is the sixth scale degree of its major scale.

Ex) The relative minor of C major is A minor.

A Natural minor scale

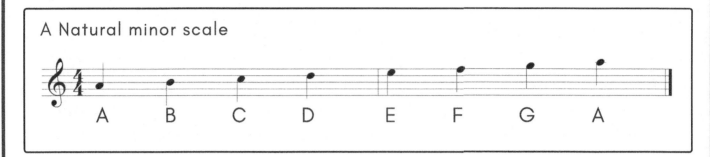

2. Harmonic minor

The 7th of the harmonic minor scale is raised by a half step.

A Harmonic minor scale

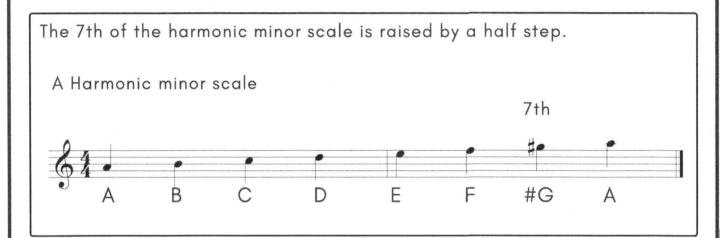

3. Melodic minor

The melodic minor scale is a minor scale with raised 6th and 7th scale degrees, but only when ascending. A descending melodic minor scale is the same as its natural minor scale.

Ascending A melodic minor scale
A   B   C   D   E   #F #G A

Descending A melodic minor scale
A   G   F   E   D   C   B   A

What are the twelve musical keys?

A, A#/B♭, B, C, C#/D♭, D, D#/E♭,
E, F, F#/G♭, G, G#/A♭

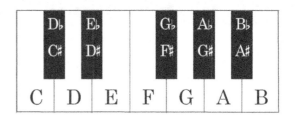

What is the circle of fifths?

The Circle of Fifths is a way to visualize twelve musical keys and arrange them in a convenient order. Each key is a fifth interval away from the next on the circle.

The circle of Fifths

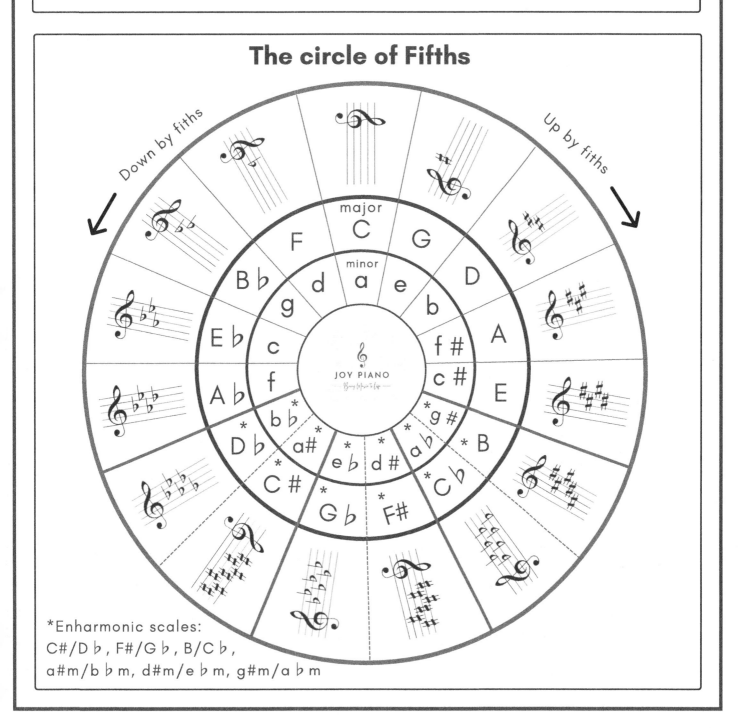

*Enharmonic scales:
C#/D♭, F#/G♭, B/C♭,
a#m/b♭m, d#m/e♭m, g#m/a♭m

C MAJOR & A MINOR

PRACTICE MUSICALLY, PLAY IT EVENLY WITHOUT ANY
EXCESSIVE TENSION, AND MEMORIZE THE SCALES.

C MAJOR

- RIGHT HAND

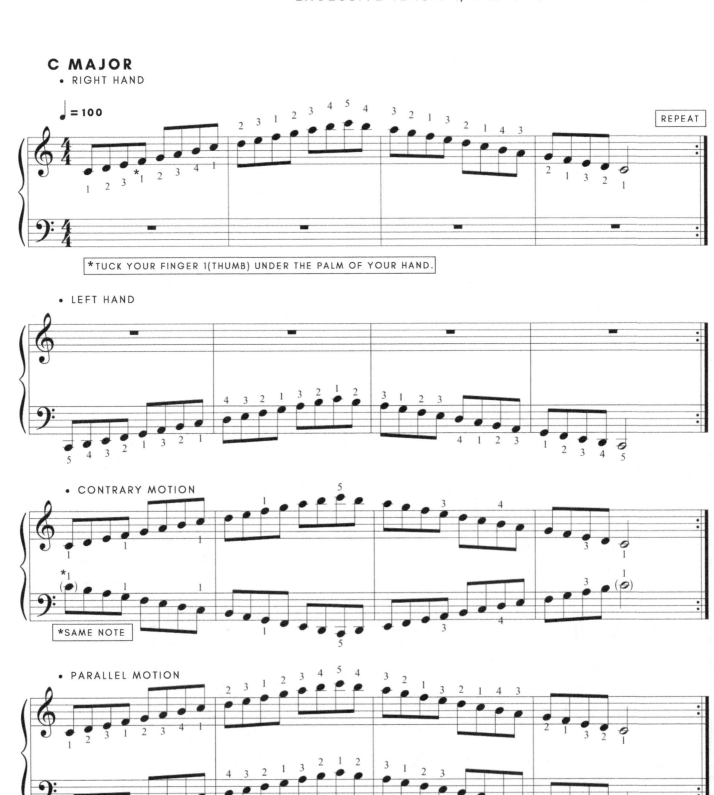

*TUCK YOUR FINGER 1(THUMB) UNDER THE PALM OF YOUR HAND.

- LEFT HAND

- CONTRARY MOTION

*SAME NOTE

- PARALLEL MOTION

A NATURAL MINOR

- RIGHT HAND

- LEFT HAND

- CONTRARY MOTION

- PARALLEL MOTION

A HARMONIC MINOR

- RIGHT HAND

*RAISED SEVENTH

9

A MELODIC MINOR

* RIGHT HAND

*RAISED SIXTH AND SEVENTH

THE SAME AS A NATURAL MINOR

G MAJOR & E MINOR

PRACTICE MUSICALLY, PLAY IT EVENLY WITHOUT ANY
EXCESSIVE TENSION, AND MEMORIZE THE SCALES.

G MAJOR

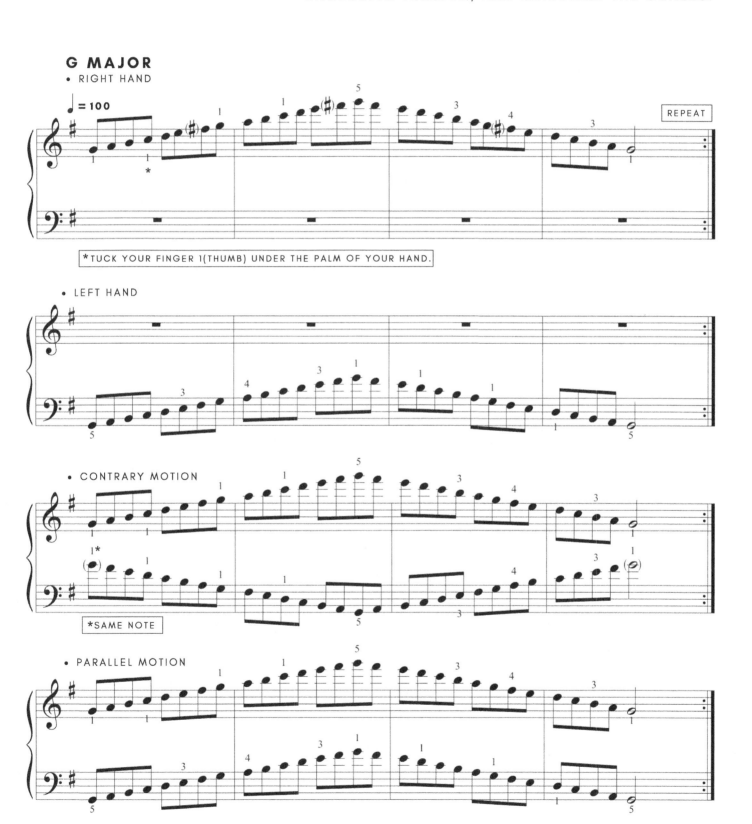

*TUCK YOUR FINGER 1(THUMB) UNDER THE PALM OF YOUR HAND.

*SAME NOTE

E NATURAL MINOR

E HARMONIC MINOR

*RAISED SEVENTH

- LEFT HAND

- PARALLEL MOTION

E MELODIC MINOR

- RIGHT HAND

*RAISED SIXTH AND SEVENTH

THE SAME AS E NATURAL MINOR

- LEFT HAND

- PARALLEL MOTION

F MAJOR & D MINOR

PRACTICE MUSICALLY, PLAY IT EVENLY WITHOUT ANY
EXCESSIVE TENSION, AND MEMORIZE THE SCALES.

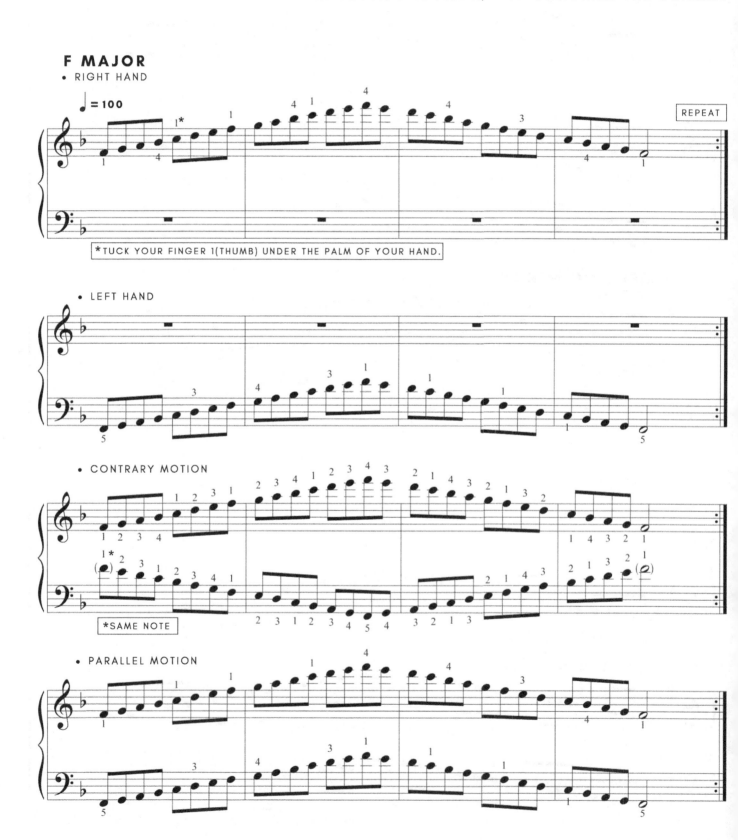

F MAJOR
- RIGHT HAND

*TUCK YOUR FINGER 1(THUMB) UNDER THE PALM OF YOUR HAND.

- LEFT HAND

- CONTRARY MOTION

*SAME NOTE

- PARALLEL MOTION

D NATURAL MINOR

* RIGHT HAND

* LEFT HAND

* CONTRARY MOTION

* PARALLEL MOTION

D HARMONIC MINOR

* RIGHT HAND

*RAISED SEVENTH

D MAJOR & B MINOR

PRACTICE MUSICALLY, PLAY IT EVENLY WITHOUT ANY EXCESSIVE TENSION, AND MEMORIZE THE SCALES.

D MAJOR
- RIGHT HAND

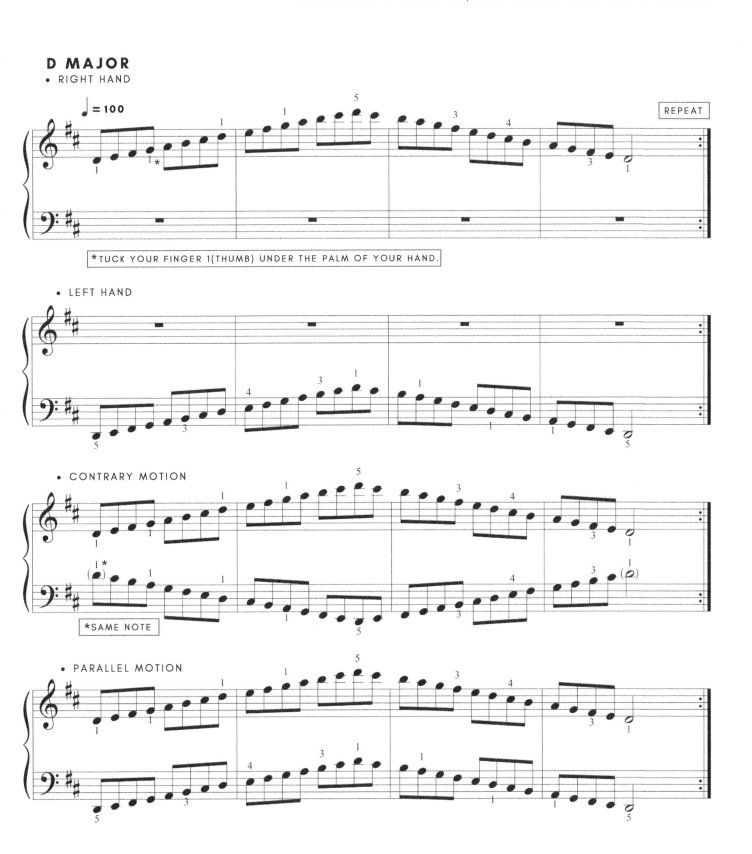

*TUCK YOUR FINGER 1(THUMB) UNDER THE PALM OF YOUR HAND.

- LEFT HAND

- CONTRARY MOTION

*SAME NOTE

- PARALLEL MOTION

B NATURAL MINOR

• RIGHT HAND

• LEFT HAND

• CONTRARY MOTION

• PARALLEL MOTION

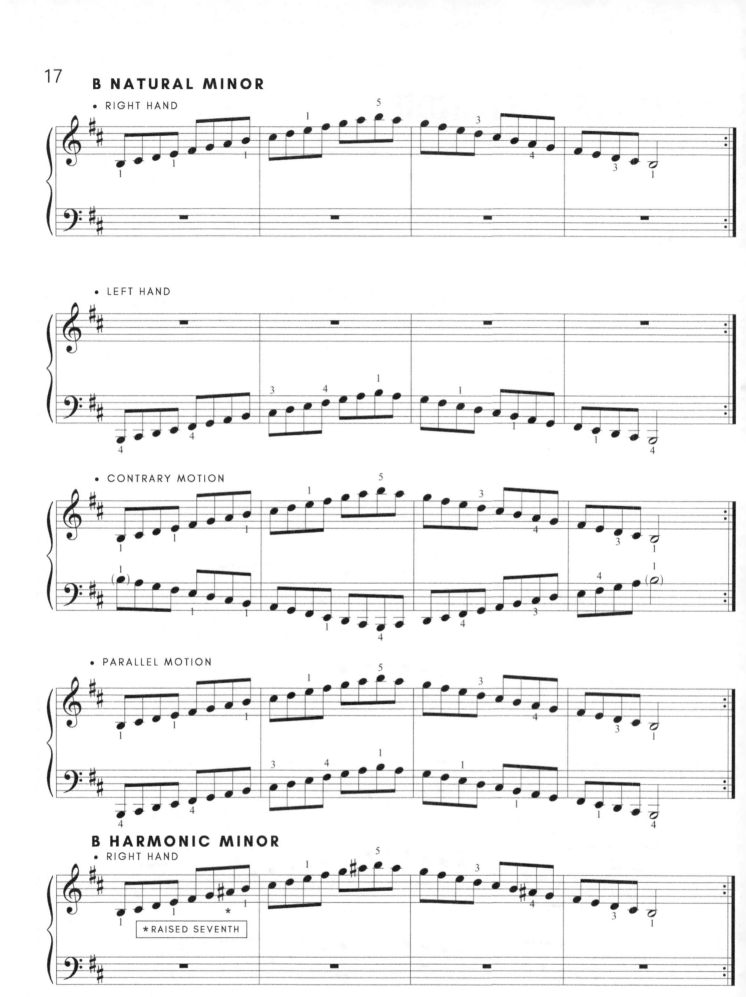

B HARMONIC MINOR

• RIGHT HAND

*RAISED SEVENTH

- LEFT HAND

- PARALLEL MOTION

B MELODIC MINOR

- RIGHT HAND

*RAISED SIXTH AND SEVENTH

THE SAME AS B NATURAL MINOR

- LEFT HAND

- PARALLEL MOTION

19

B♭ MAJOR & G MINOR

PRACTICE MUSICALLY, PLAY IT EVENLY WITHOUT ANY
EXCESSIVE TENSION, AND MEMORIZE THE SCALES.

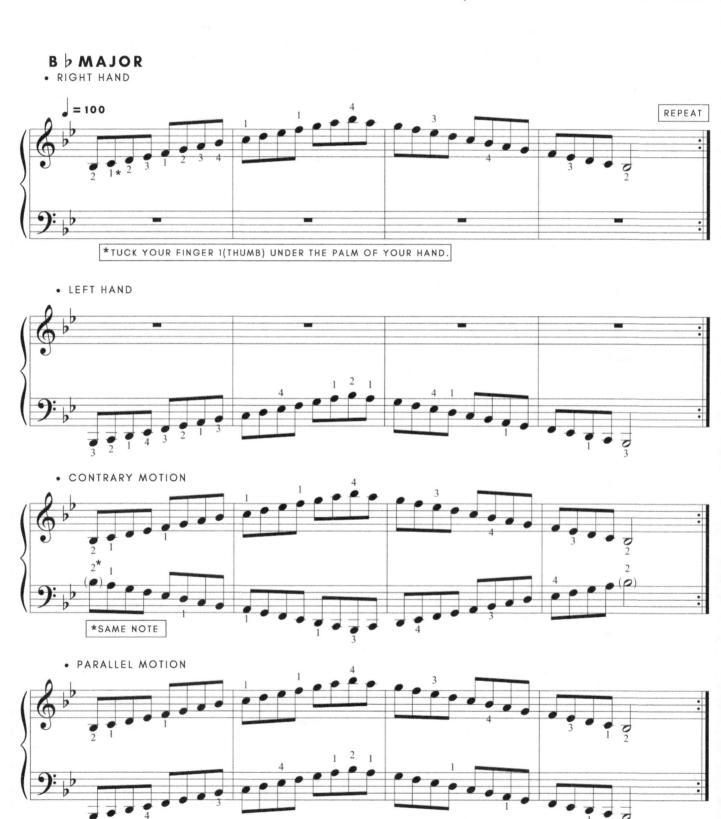

G NATURAL MINOR

- RIGHT HAND

- LEFT HAND

- CONTRARY MOTION

- PARALLEL MOTION

G HARMONIC MINOR

- RIGHT HAND

*RAISED SEVENTH

21

G MELODIC MINOR

* RIGHT HAND

*RAISED SIXTH AND SEVENTH

THE SAME AS G NATURAL MINOR

A MAJOR & F# MINOR

PRACTICE MUSICALLY, PLAY IT EVENLY WITHOUT ANY
EXCESSIVE TENSION, AND MEMORIZE THE SCALES.

A MAJOR

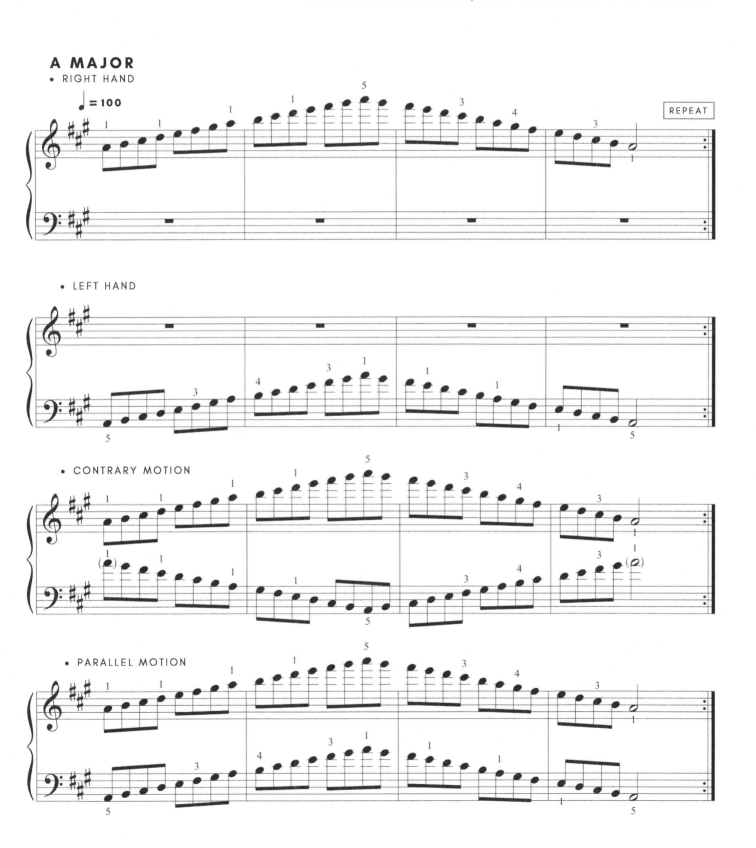

23   F# NATURAL MINOR

- RIGHT HAND

- LEFT HAND

- CONTRARY MOTION

- PARALLEL MOTION

F# HARMONIC MINOR

- RIGHT HAND

- LEFT HAND

- PARALLEL MOTION

F# MELODIC MINOR

- RIGHT HAND

- LEFT HAND

- PARALLEL MOTION

E♭ MAJOR & C MINOR

PRACTICE MUSICALLY, PLAY IT EVENLY WITHOUT ANY
EXCESSIVE TENSION, AND MEMORIZE THE SCALES.

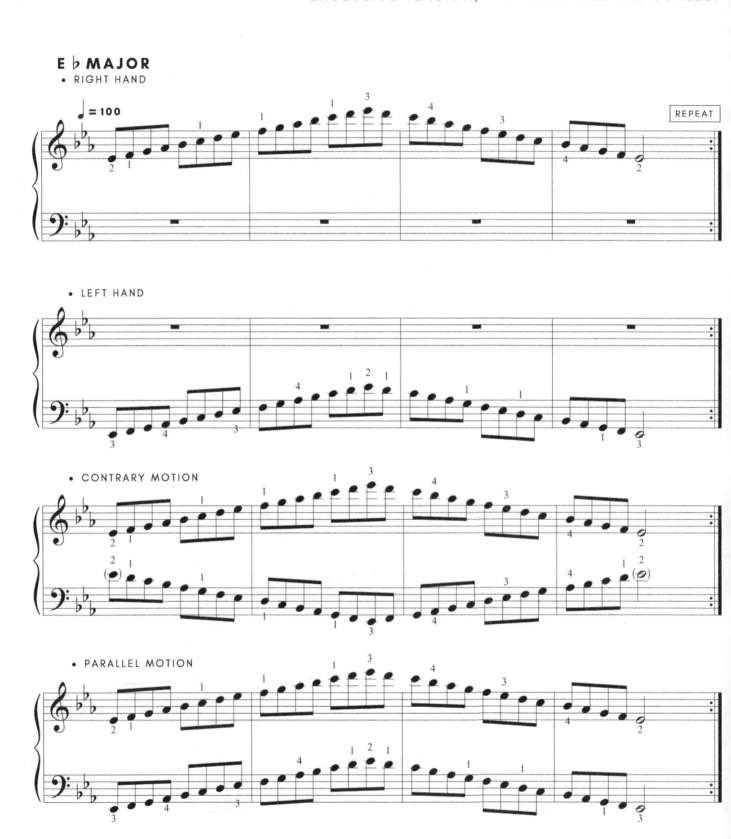

C NATURAL MINOR

- RIGHT HAND

- LEFT HAND

- CONTRARY MOTION

- PARALLEL MOTION

C HARMONIC MINOR

- RIGHT HAND

27

E MAJOR & C# MINOR

PRACTICE MUSICALLY, PLAY IT EVENLY WITHOUT ANY
EXCESSIVE TENSION, AND MEMORIZE THE SCALES.

E MAJOR
- RIGHT HAND

- LEFT HAND

- CONTRARY MOTION

- PARALLEL MOTION

C# NATURAL MINOR

- RIGHT HAND

- LEFT HAND

- CONTRARY MOTION

- PARALLEL MOTION

C# HARMONIC MINOR

- RIGHT HAND

- LEFT HAND

- PARALLEL MOTION

C# MELODIC MINOR

- RIGHT HAND

- LEFT HAND

- PARALLEL MOTION

A♭ MAJOR & F MINOR

PRACTICE MUSICALLY, PLAY IT EVENLY WITHOUT ANY
EXCESSIVE TENSION, AND MEMORIZE THE SCALES.

A♭ MAJOR

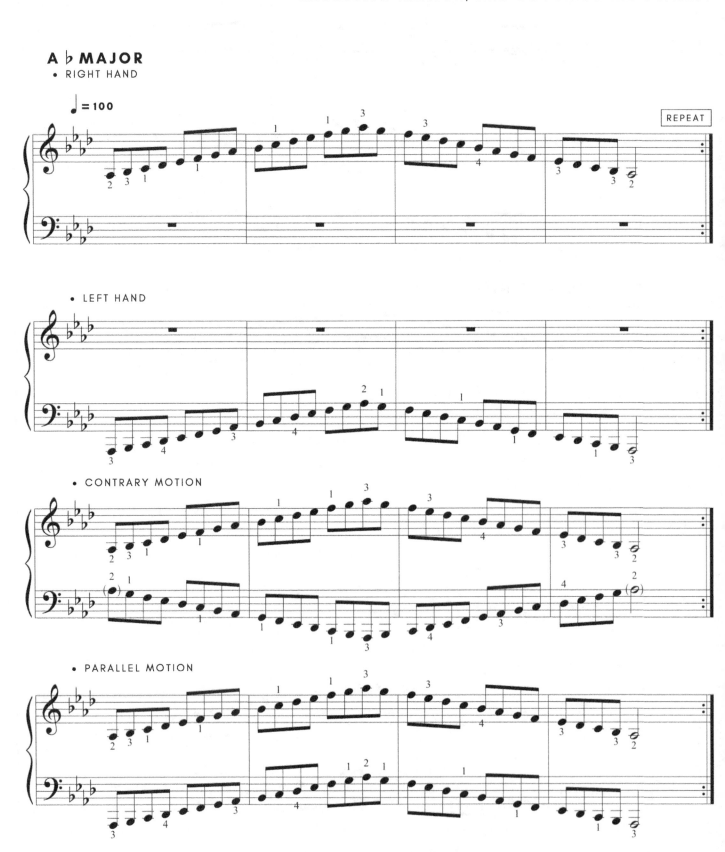

F NATURAL MINOR

- RIGHT HAND

- LEFT HAND

- CONTRARY MOTION

- PARALLEL MOTION

F HARMONIC MINOR

- RIGHT HAND

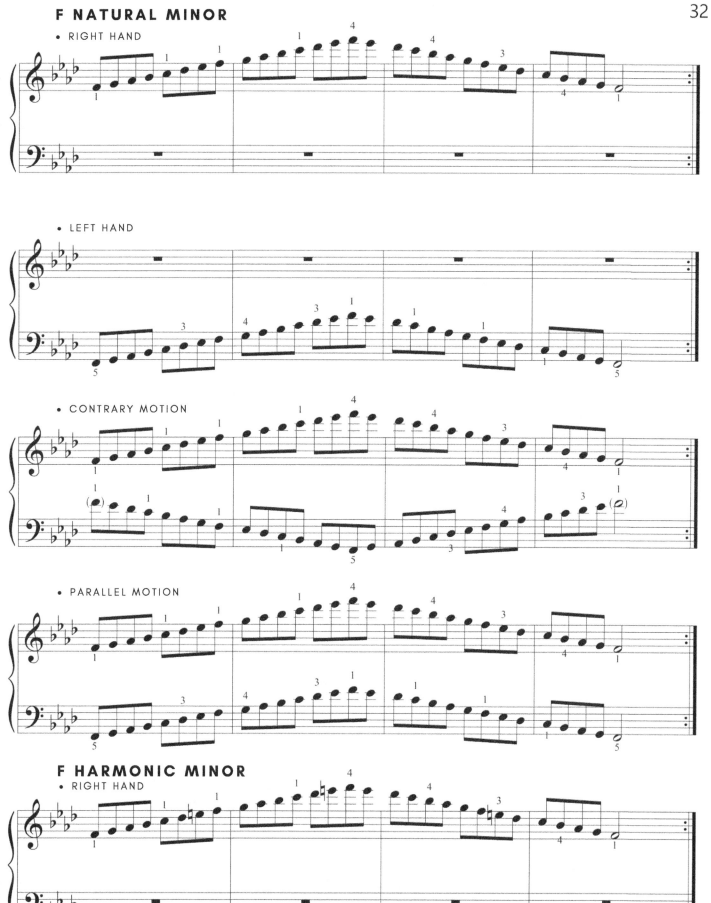

• LEFT HAND

• PARALLEL MOTION

F MELODIC MINOR

• RIGHT HAND

• LEFT HAND

• PARALLEL MOTION

B MAJOR & G# MINOR

PRACTICE MUSICALLY, PLAY IT EVENLY WITHOUT ANY
EXCESSIVE TENSION, AND MEMORIZE THE SCALES.

B MAJOR
- RIGHT HAND

- LEFT HAND

- CONTRARY MOTION

- PARALLEL MOTION

35 G# NATURAL MINOR

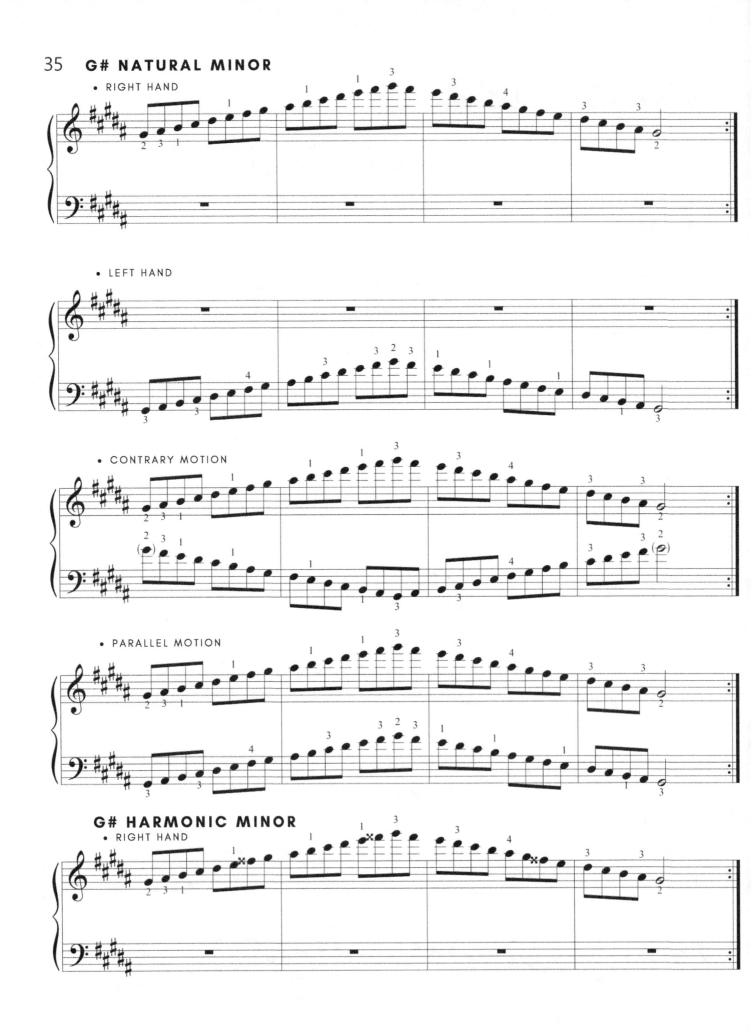

- LEFT HAND

- PARALLEL MOTION

G# MELODIC MINOR

- RIGHT HAND

- LEFT HAND

- PARALLEL MOTION

D♭ MAJOR & B♭ MINOR

PRACTICE MUSICALLY, PLAY IT EVENLY WITHOUT ANY
EXCESSIVE TENSION, AND MEMORIZE THE SCALES.

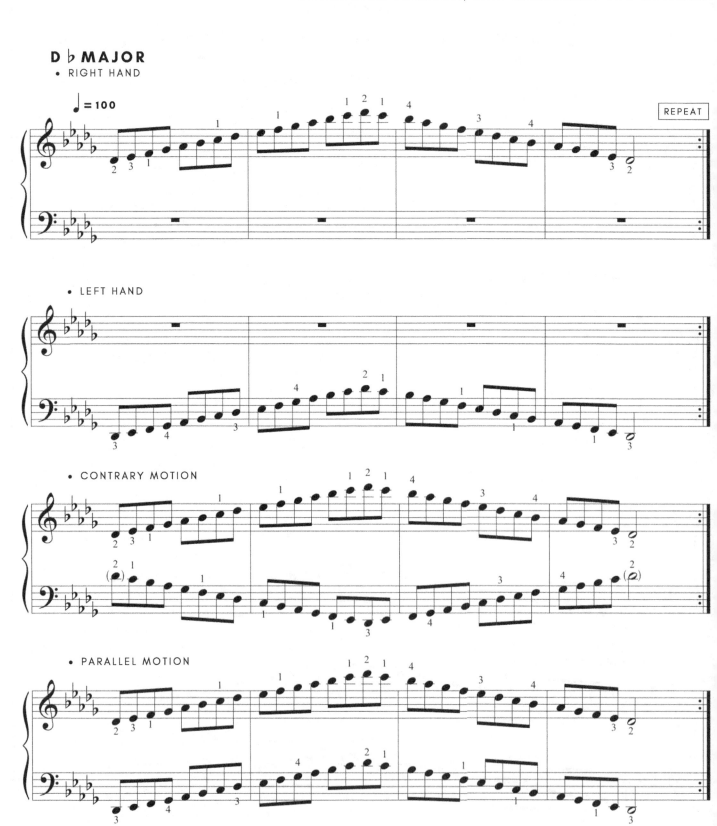

B♭ NATURAL MINOR

- RIGHT HAND

- LEFT HAND

- CONTRARY MOTION

- PARALLEL MOTION

B♭ HARMONIC MINOR

- RIGHT HAND

- LEFT HAND

- PARALLEL MOTION

B♭ MELODIC MINOR

- RIGHT HAND

- LEFT HAND

- PARALLEL MOTION

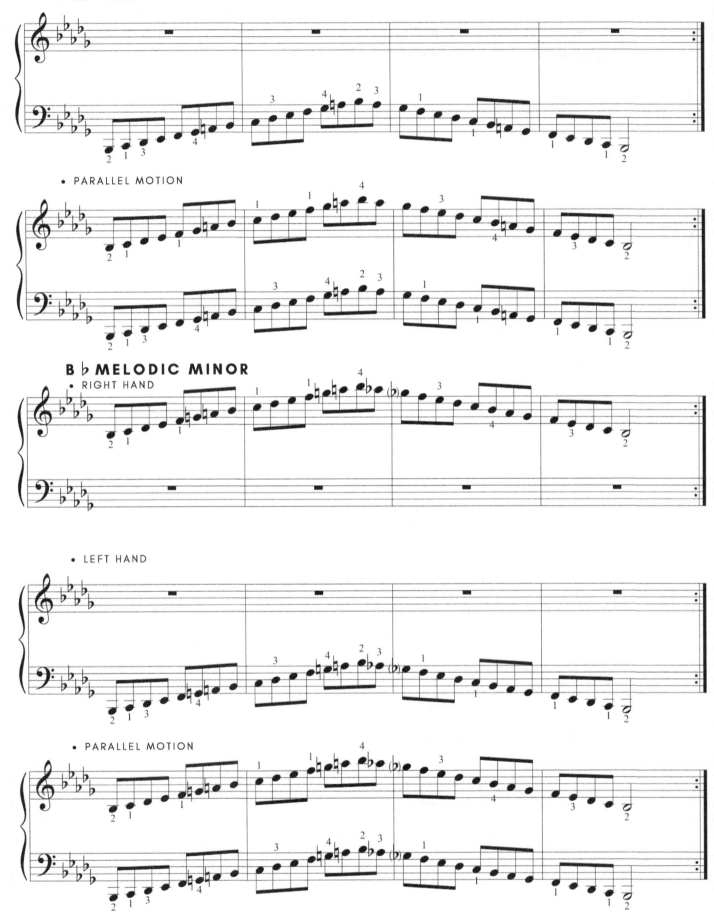

F# MAJOR & D# MINOR

PRACTICE MUSICALLY, PLAY IT EVENLY WITHOUT ANY
EXCESSIVE TENSION, AND MEMORIZE THE SCALES.

F# MAJOR

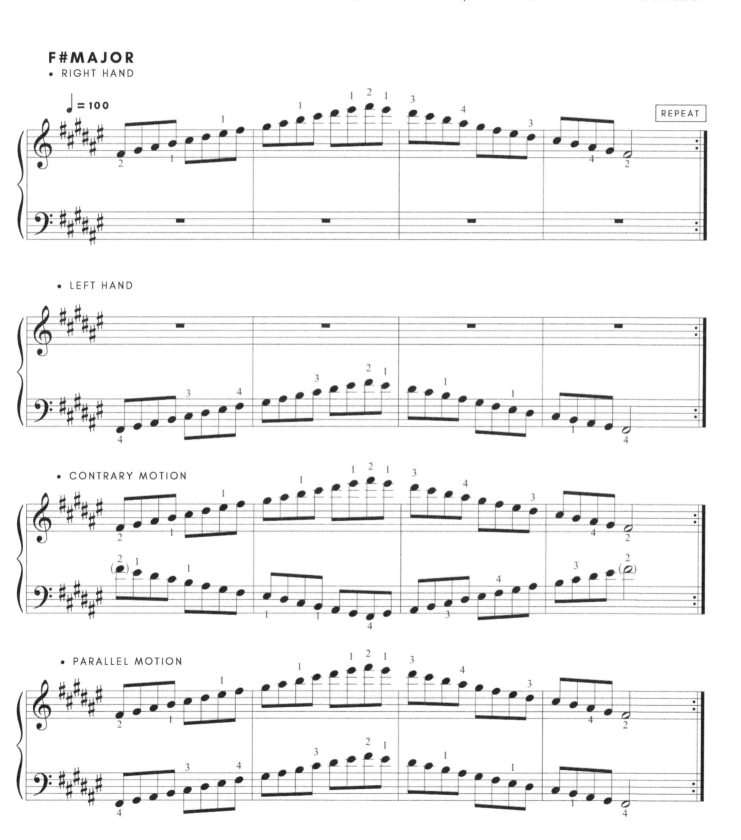

D# NATURAL MINOR

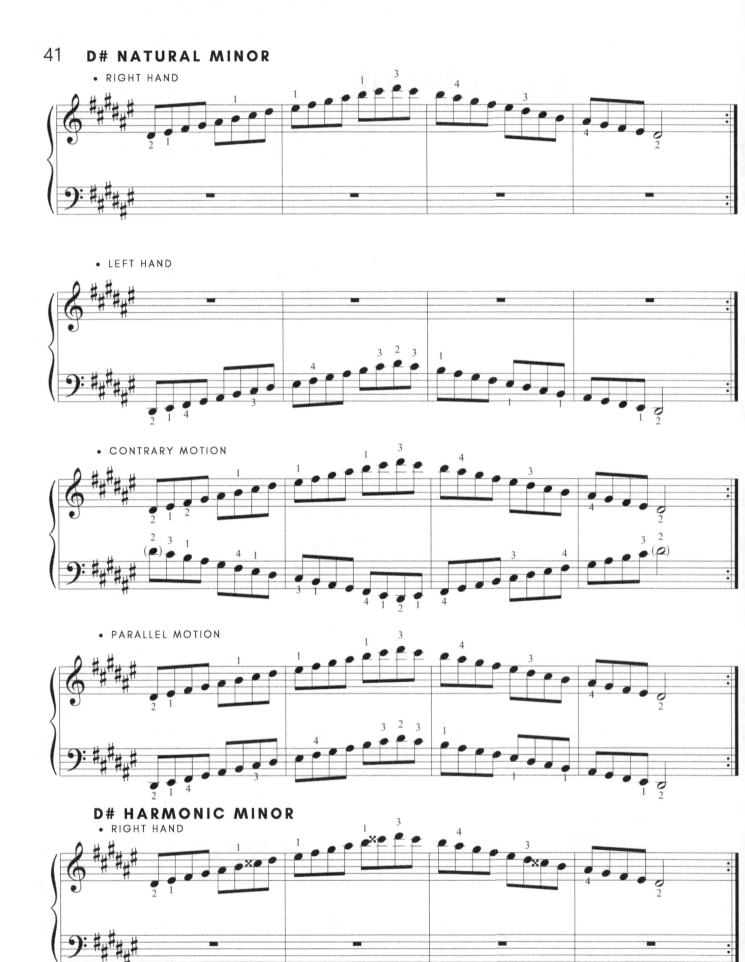

D# MELODIC MINOR

G♭ MAJOR & E♭ MINOR

PRACTICE MUSICALLY, PLAY IT EVENLY WITHOUT ANY
EXCESSIVE TENSION, AND MEMORIZE THE SCALES.

G♭ MAJOR

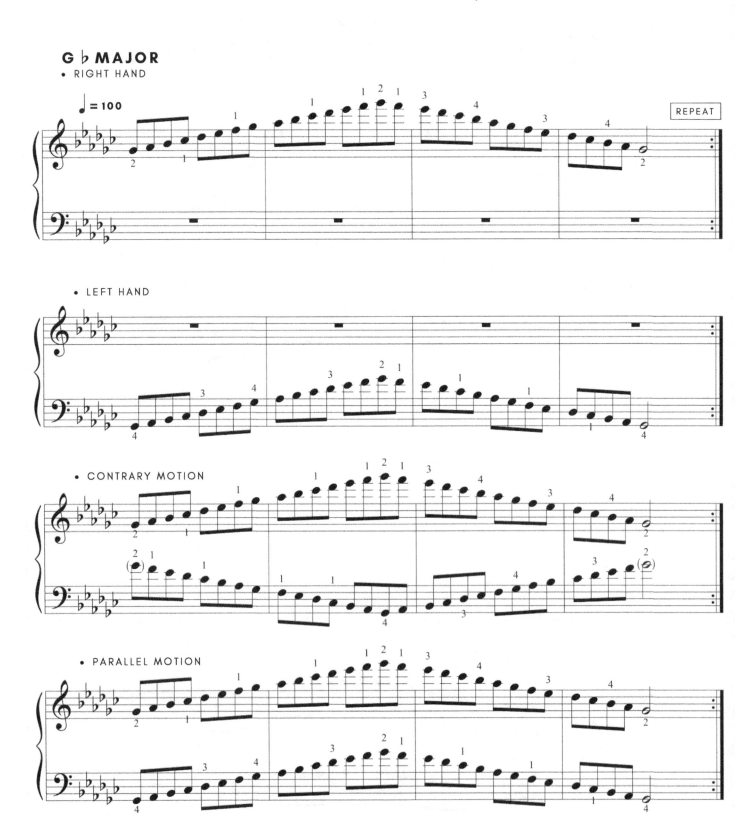

E♭ NATURAL MINOR

- RIGHT HAND

- LEFT HAND

- CONTRARY MOTION

- PARALLEL MOTION

E♭ HARMONIC MINOR

- RIGHT HAND

E♭ MELODIC MINOR

C# MAJOR & A# MINOR

PRACTICE MUSICALLY, PLAY IT EVENLY WITHOUT ANY
EXCESSIVE TENSION, AND MEMORIZE THE SCALES.

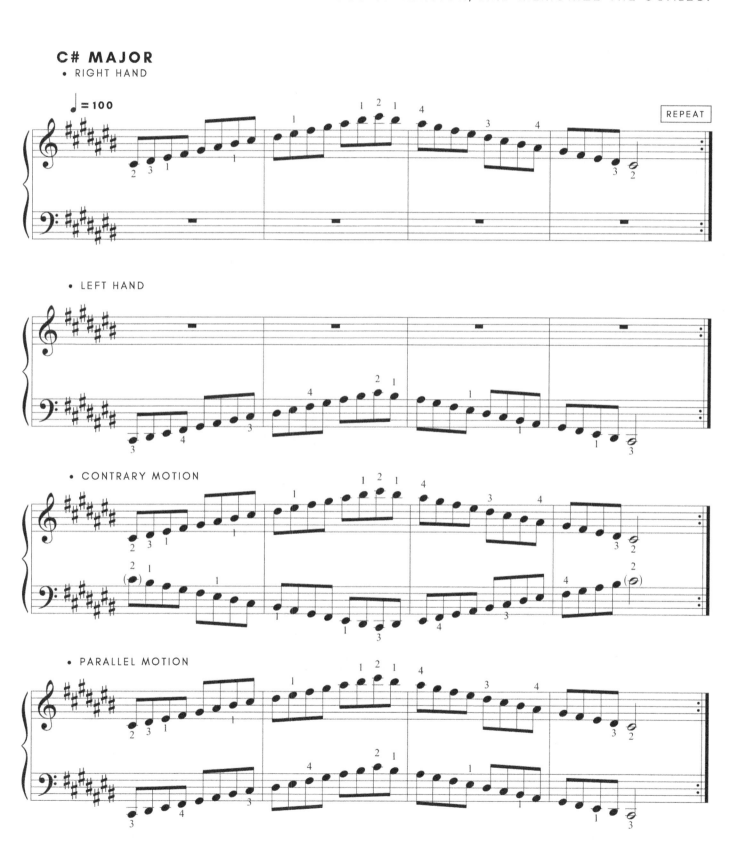

A# NATURAL MINOR

A# MELODIC MINOR

C♭ MAJOR & A♭ MINOR

PRACTICE MUSICALLY, PLAY IT EVENLY WITHOUT ANY
EXCESSIVE TENSION, AND MEMORIZE THE SCALES.

C♭ MAJOR
- RIGHT HAND

- LEFT HAND

- CONTRARY MOTION

- PARALLEL MOTION

A♭ NATURAL MINOR

- RIGHT HAND

- LEFT HAND

- CONTRARY MOTION

- PARALLEL MOTION

A♭ HARMONIC MINOR

- RIGHT HAND

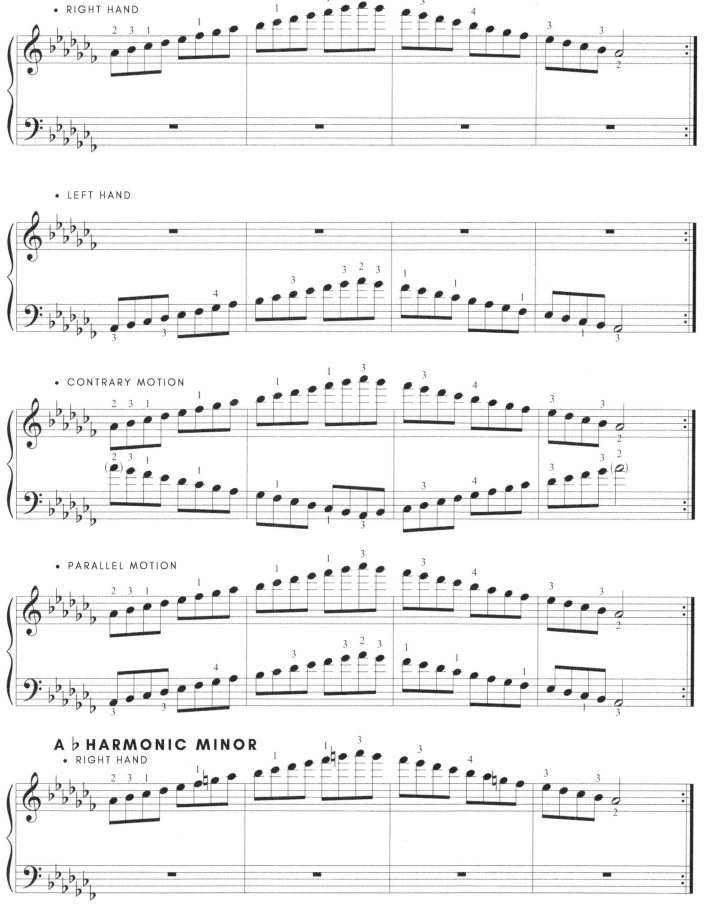

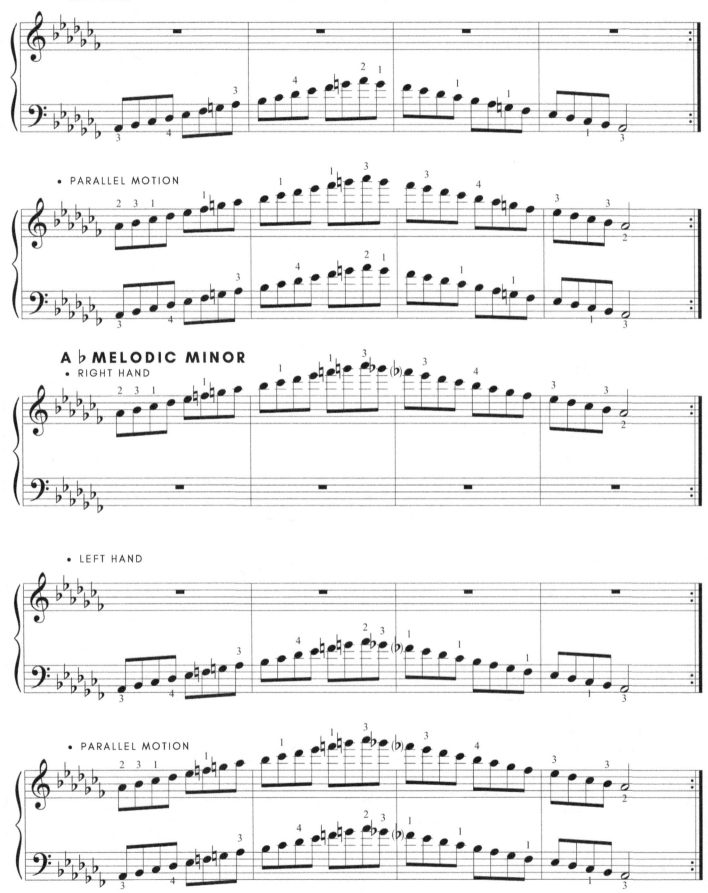

A♭ MELODIC MINOR

JOY PIANO

Bring Music to Life

Made in the USA
Las Vegas, NV
21 April 2024

88962067R00031